My Journey

in the

CHARISMATIC RENEWAL

My Journey

in the

CHARISMATIC RENEWAL

Linda Jones

Copyright © 2007-2020 by Linda K. Jones

Published by Yowza Publishing
YowzaPublishing.com

ISBN: 978-1-951410-02-5

Version 2.0.0

Printing: 10 9 8 7 6 5 4 3 2 1

Cover Image by Pexels from Pixabay

All rights reserved. No part of this publication may be reproduced, stored in a retrieval system, or transmitted in any form or by any means without prior written permission of the publisher. The only exception is brief quotations in printed reviews.

CONTENTS

Charismatic Renewal .... - 1 -
THERE HAS TO BE MORE TO LIFE
THAN THIS .... - 5 -
THE LIGHT BEGINS TO DAWN .... - 13 -
JESUS BECOMES REAL TO US .... - 17 -
OUR LIFESTYLE CHANGES .... - 23 -
MY EXPERIENCE .... - 27 -
THE OUTPOURING EXPANDS .... - 29 -
PREACHING THE GOSPEL PUBLICALLY .... - 35 -
TAKING JESUS TO THE SUBURBS .... - 43 -
DANVILLE: A NEW AREA OF OUTREACH .... - 47 -
SPIRITUAL WARFARE .... - 53 -
INDIANAPOLIS .... - 55 -
BACK TO ILLINOIS .... - 59 -
TEACH AND BE TAUGHT IN MISSOURI .... - 61 -
OUR WORK AS HOME MISSIONARIES .... - 67 -
THE WESTCOVE PROPERTY .... - 71 -
THE WIND OF THE SPIRIT CHANGES .... - 85 -
A NEW WAVE .... - 87 -
The Four Spiritual Laws .... - 91 -
Holy Spirit Baptism .... - 93 -

Charismatic Renewal

In 1968, we did not realize that we were part of a sovereign move of the Holy Spirit of God that would affect the entire earth. This movement, called the Charismatic Movement, was the beginning of a revival that would take the Baptism in the Holy Spirit, or Pentecostal experience to thousands and even millions of people across the United States and to the ends of the world. This super-natural Holy Spirit movement changed the lives of people from all denominations as well as many unchurched people who accepted Jesus straight from the streets.

Back then there were many nights I spent worrying and wondering where my husband was. Was this going to be our lot in life? Greg, our nine-year old, was starting to get into trouble. A man had called and complained that he and a neighbor boy had gotten into his grain to play. With three boys, I did not want to continue to have to handle these problems, and what did the future hold? Would it get worse?

I am so thankful that God intervened in our lives when He did. My passion for Jesus has not diminished over the years, and it is because I have seen that He is a good God. Life has trials and tribulations, because we are not in heaven yet, but God's kingdom is secure. As a part of that kingdom, my relationship with Jesus is my Rock, and I have learned principles that have not only blessed my life but changes the lives of all who will listen to the Word. Even as I write, we have a grandson with a terrible disease, and we are praying for healing. I rest in the love and the grace the Lord has for each and every one of us.

The culture of the sixties was greatly affected by a rebellion against society which manifest in the Hippie movement. The new availability of illegal drugs, illicit sex, called "free love" and rebellion against authority played a large part in this change, and it began in the youth culture. As I look back, I can see parallels between the Spirit of God working through the Charismatic Movement to expand the kingdom of God and the spirit of Satan working in the lives of unbelievers to spread his culture, or kingdom, of darkness. Satan has a goal to take as many as possible to hell with him, and drugs opened the door for his last day's onslaught against mankind. God's Spirit was at work to establish His kingdom through those who believe in His dear Son.

In the late sixties and early seventies, the Charismatic Revival was often called the Jesus Movement. This was because many who accepted Christ were young people and many, like those in the hippie movement, were looking for answers to give meaning to life. The real meaning in life comes from Jesus who has a wonderful plan for every person. I praise the Lord that we are a part of God's family and His plan for our generation. The reason that this Pentecostal outpouring was called the Charismatic Renewal is because a great emphasis was on put the gifts of the Holy Spirit, or charisma of God. In the Greek it is spelled *charisma* which means divine gift.

My husband and my testimonies are typical of so many people who were a part of the Charismatic Movement, and that is why I thought a testimony of our journey with Christ during those years would be worth putting on paper. Looking backward over the years we see a different perspective than when we were living them. We were just striving to serve the Lord, and we were so in awe of the reality of the Holy Spirit.

History proves that the sixties and seventies did produce a supernatural, sovereign, move of God's Spirit in the United States that eventually spread around the world. Our part in this spiritual awakening, Jerry and mine, began in Tolono, Illinois, a small town just south of Champaign-Urbana.

THERE HAS TO BE MORE TO LIFE THAN THIS

First, I want to lay some groundwork as to how it began. At that time, I was twenty-eight years old, married for ten years and had three sons. Greg was nine, Charles four and Brad three. My life centered around a beauty shop in my home, a social and service group that I and most of my friends belonged to in Champaign, and my family who lived about fifty miles away in Rossville. Rossville was a small town that I had spent my entire childhood in. Between the house, the business, the kids, friends, and family I was "living life." Religion had a small part in my life, very small, and Jesus was an unknown entity in my life even though I did occasionally go to church.

I was raised in a home that was not centered on church. However, my parents had both been raised around strong Christian values like most in that era. They had Methodist and German Apostolic roots in their family backgrounds. As a child, I remember my mother donating goods to church fund raising events, and I remember her going to church a few times. She always decorated our bikes and made great costumes for the church's Fall Festival Parade. I went to the local Methodist church off and on because my friends went, and we were active in the high school youth group because of a high school teacher's influence. I had gone through confirmation as a pre-teen and joined the church, sang in the children's choir, etc. However, my church attendance as a child growing up was very sporadic. Many families were more committed to church, but we did not consider ourselves heathens.

I thought I had the best childhood ever. I loved my family and while I was academically an average student, my best friends excelled, and we pretty much had a good time attending and participating in all the school activities. During those years, schools were run with the same rules and ethics that Christian schools are today. We had a dress code and the teachers would never have been seen in a bar. Teachers were expected to live by the same moral standards that ministers are today. However, I remember many times being sad during my high school years, and I believe it was the spiritual void in my life that caused these feelings.

Religion was not talked about except on very rare occasions among my peers. I belonged to a group of girls who called ourselves the BABS. I won't tell you what it stood for because it was not ladylike, but we thought it was very hip, and we were the in crowd. We were typical teen-agers learning to rock and roll to "Rock around the Clock" and do the things of the late fifties. Elvis was on the Ed Sullivan Show, and my dad said he was a dope fiend. (That term did not last long.) My friends and I loved him and Pat Boone. I bought a skirt at Kay's which was the original poodle skirt. The way I remember it was expensive, but no one at that time knew it would be a fashion statement of the era. We BABS bleached our bangs as a symbol that we belonged, and we all make shirts out of two red bandanas sewn together. (To be that size again!) Anyway, life in Rossville was very safe and slow on the whole.

Now it was the sixties and things were changing….FAST. Jerry and I were moving with the times. While drugs were not a part of our lives, alcohol was. I had grown up with a bar in the home and as teenagers my friends and I had drank some, but none of us really liked it all that much. After I was married, the friends I had were pretty much the same way. We all drank socially, but our goals were more on materialism and getting bigger and better homes. The gang we ran with were good people and many of our friends were very successful for young adults. They attended church, some more than others, but as far as I knew, they were not born-again.

We had moved from Champaign, Illinois to Tolono because we had found a house big enough for our family and a beauty shop. Having grown up in a small town, I thought it would be good for the kids, and I liked the quieter life. It was still within easy driving distance to Champaign.

Sheila, my best friend at the time, told me she had an ex-boyfriend who owned an implement business in Tolono. She said she had heard that he had become religious! I thought, "Well I'm religious, too, so what?!" Little did I know. At that time I seldom went to church and did not have a clue as to what true Biblical Christianity was all about.

I liked my house. It was a big old house on Main Street, and my mother, Jerry and I papered and painted and put in the beauty shop. I attended the local Methodist Church, more to meet people than for any other reason. I met Jim, Sheila's friend, along with Bill, a guy who we knew from Champaign. I was surprised at Bill being there. We had met Bill and his wife at a social event in Champaign. Bill owned the local bowling alley in Champaign, but I was surprised that he was in church and especially in Tolono.

The Tolono Methodist preacher was an ex-Navy man

who had gotten radically saved while in the Navy. Later I found out that he was the instrument God used to bring Jim and Bill into a born-again experience. As a Methodist at that time, my theology was, I hoped that if God was real, and if there was a heaven, He would let me in. Really, I did not give the whole matter much thought. Usually I went to church to ease a guilty conscience for not going to church. I guess somewhere I thought it was a good thing, so I had some kind of abstract belief in God. I had taken confirmation and been sprinkled in Jr. High School along with my friends, and I did not know there was any more out there to do to be a Christian. I did not call myself a Christian. I called myself a Methodist.

However, Jerry had no faith, and it irritated him to death when I nagged him to go with me to church. On rare occasions he would go, but the arguing about it was horrible beforehand, and since I went so rarely myself, I wonder why I fussed with him about it.

We had met when I was fifteen and Jerry was seventeen. He had brought a friend, Jim to Rossville to look for a girl Jim had just met. It just so happened that Judy and I were walking down the street together and that is how Jerry and I met. Judy and Jim later were married, and she became a Spirit-filled believer a few years after we did.

Jerry had gone to Boy Scout camp with my brother, Richard, and he knew that Richard had a sister. He had decided to see if he could check out this sister, so he was glad to meet me. I trust this was providence! Anyway, I thought he was the cutest guy I had ever met. Our marriage truly was made in heaven, because without God we would never have made it. Jerry has always been my favorite person to be with, and for that I am very

Charismatic Renewal

thankful. I appreciate his walk with Jesus and his servant heart. However, that is now. Back then he had some major issues.

Jerry went to the Marine Corp after his graduation, and I finished high school. My brother and sister-in-law had eloped to Mississippi where there was no waiting period to get married, and so when I graduated and Jerry was on leave, we did the same. I was not quite eighteen.

Now, three kids and ten years later, we were in need of the Lord. Our marriage was beginning to be on the rocks. Jerry was staying out later and later many nights after work and spending way too much time in the bars. He was raised an only child by a widowed mother. Many of his relatives were alcoholics, and even as a teen-ager he had been exposed to too much alcohol. Unlike me, Jerry liked the stuff. It was beginning to be a real problem in our marriage. I remember thinking that I did not want to get a divorce, because my grandma had told me that if you remarried you would be committing adultery. Even as an unbeliever, I must have had some fear of God because I really was tired of not trusting my husband, but divorce was not an option. A good thing is that these problems probably softened my heart to hear the gospel.

About this same time some friends of my parents, who had always seemed like the perfect married couple, got a divorce. Eileen had left her husband for the professor she was working for at the University of Illinois. That, along with our problems, was shaking my world which before had always seemed secure. This was back in the late sixties when divorce was still pretty much of a rarity.

I look back, from a Christian perspective, and I can see that when growing up, my family was not perfect. My dad also was a drinker and a gambler, and he was not present in the home much of the time. He owned a trucking company, and he spent his weekend and most evenings at the Country Club or a favorite business hang out. He was not a golfer but played cards. My mother managed to make our life seem normal. As the whole, dad provided well for the family. Mom never complained about having to be both mom and dad in many situations, and I had great respect for them both. However, I know much stress was put on mother, and she was a great example on how a woman can provide a stable home in an unstable situation if she puts her mind to it for the well-being of the children.

When my dad went to be with the Lord, there was a huge crowd at the funeral. He had a stroke and died at the age of sixty-four. Hard living shortened his life. I often think he could have been dynamite in the Lord's work, because people listened to him. Mother would get aggravated that people would hang on his words, which is about the only criticism I remember her saying about him. Dad accepted the Lord in the hospital after the stroke, and he lived for two more years. Even though he was an invalid, the transformation was obvious. Dad never drank another martini, or any other alcoholic beverage, and he never swore again. (It had been a habit.) He was a great witness to his sisters and others close to him.

It seemed like the parties we attended with our friends, were less fun. There was simply too much drinking and flirting. My best friend's husband was stepping out on her and everyone knew it but her. We played bridge with different couples, but all we could think about was getting a better house and making more money. I remember playing bridge with some girlfriends one day and telling them that when I was in high school, one guy I dated was a minister and another became a minister. They thought that was hilarious that I would date a minister. I did, too, but looking back I think God may have drawn me to those young men, and maybe was even then calling my name. I didn't REALLY date one of those guys. At fourteen, I just liked him, as girls do boys at that age, and he invited me to church with him one Sunday. I remember being embarrassed because I could not find the scriptures in the Bible during Sunday school, and he had to help me. I dated the other young man when Jerry was gone to the service. He was a minister in a small Christian Church close to Rossville. I was only seventeen, so he must have been terribly young. He liked me, but I was already too smitten with Jerry to get really interested in anyone else.

I was feeling unrest. Many of our friends were building new homes, having kids, and enjoying life as we knew it, but I was wondering if this was all there was to life. We rented the upstairs of a local bar in downtown Tolono to have a private party, and I remember some of the leading people at the Methodist church were there. Drinking and partying along with the best of us. I really did not think that was strange, because I, a church member, was hosting it. It was what people did. Go to church and live for self, wasn't it?!

THE LIGHT BEGINS TO DAWN

Remember Jim? My friend Sheila's ex-boyfriend who had gotten religious?! Well, his sister, Mary, was a regular customer in my beauty shop, and she told me about a book I needed to read called, Cross and the Switchblade. During this time other women also witnessed to me in the beauty shop. Two sisters, Judy and Janet, talked to me about the Lord. They had been raised in the Catholic Church and lived in a very poor and abusive home while growing up, and they had had some pretty rough experiences. They both were married with small children and really wanted a better life for their children... Judy, the youngest was just nineteen and had a three-year old. She became a special friend during this time as she shared her faith. They came into the shop thumping their Bibles. They had begun to go to Webber Street Church of Christ. They stressed that it was a New Testament church, and they were so were excited to learn that the Bible was absolute truth. They had not learned this as Catholic children.

Please do not think I am slamming different churches. This is just my testimony from my experiences and the experiences of my friends in their journeys of faith in Christ. I had not been raised to believe that the Bible was absolute truth, and I'm sure their testimony influenced me as I began my walk in the Word. Judy had three children and later two of Judy's children became doctors, and one a social worker with a master's degree. This is God's goodness in a family dedicated to Him.

Jerry came home from work with the book, <u>Cross and the Switchblade</u>. It had been given to him by a guy at work. This young man, Gene, was a backslidden Nazarene, but he had compassion for Jerry, and gave him the book. I do not know if Gene had read it or not, but later when Jerry became a Christian, Gene also returned to the Lord and became a minister in the Methodist church. At that time, Jerry did not want to read the book, so he gave it to me. It began the change in my life. It was the testimony of a young Assemblies of God preacher who God supernaturally called to minister on the streets of New York City. It was about gangs, drugs and the inner city of New York City.

I read the book and I was amazed to hear that this young minister, David Wilkerson FELT the presence of God. I had never contemplated a supernatural experience with God, the Holy Spirit. My family just did not believe in the supernatural. We were really humanists in every sense of the word, even though we would have said we were Christians (or Methodists) if you had asked what we were. The book talked about drug addicts being totally delivered from drugs by an experience with the Holy Spirit and the risen Christ. This was mind-boggling to me. And it was also the best news I ever imagined could be heard. I thought, "If we can know God then I must seek this out." Also, I was fascinated with the idea of speaking in tongues as a spiritual experience. This spiritual experience was talked about in the book, and I had never heard of such a thing or of Pentecost. I had heard about Holy Rollers, but never really thought about what that might mean.

Before this, I remember customers in the beauty shop telling me I should quit smoking and me telling them that I would have a nervous breakdown if I did. However, just before my conversion, I did quit, and it still seems a miracle that God was so gracious to me in delivering me from a bad habit that began…on the sneak…when I was as young as the sixth grade. Back in the sixties smoking was not known to be a health hazard like it is today, and many more people smoked. However, in the back of our minds we knew it was not right, along with drinking, and swearing. However, at that time, I was not convicted in the least. Also, I was not convicted about drinking. I just did not like Jerry out drinking late at night and neglecting me.

Right before I saw the light, I remember being in Sunday school and the class saying that Jesus was God. I felt like they were wrong. I thought God the Father was God, and Jesus was just a good man. The class told me to find out what grace and mercy meant. I went home and asked Jerry what they meant. Like he would know?! This was before I read <u>Cross and the Switchblade</u>. However, I did sense that something was going on with Jim and Bill in their Christian walk that I did not know about.

I also remember seeing news of the Six Day War on television in 1967. At that time, I did not equate Israel with Christianity. Needless to say, at that time I was Biblically illiterate and spiritually unenlightened. I believe it is the Spirit of the Lord that allows me to recall seeing that event on television and remembering it.

JESUS BECOMES REAL TO US

I was beginning to be spiritually hungry for God. I decided that if God spoke to people like David Wilkerson, He could speak to me. I also thought if the Bible really was true, I should read it. I did not just begin to read it, I devoured it. Day and night my nose was in the Bible. I began to study the Bible with Judy and other young mothers. We met daily from house to house, and we always had our Bibles along with a kid or two in tow. We met in our homes on Sunday evenings with people from the church, and many who came to those home meetings attended various churches in Tolono. We were drawn together by the Holy Spirit. The ex- Navy pastor left the Methodist church and Dick and Irene Garabrant replaced him. They both were about as ignorant of the working of the Holy Spirit as the rest of us, but they were open.

After reading the Cross and the Switchblade and seeing in the Bible a clear teaching on the Baptism in the Holy Spirit and speaking in tongues, I brought it up at the home meeting on Sunday night. Some said it was not for today, even though they too liked the book. I still to this day do not understand how people read the Bible and pick and choose what they want to apply to their lives. But again, it takes the Holy Spirit's revelation to see truth.

However, one lady in the Sunday night Bible study, Ruth, said she had spoken in tongues. At that time no one else in the group seemed too interested but I immediately wanted to hear her story. I can't tell you how overjoyed I was to meet a real live person with this experience. Ruth was excited that I was excited.

A couple from Villa Grove had taken Ruth to a Full Gospel Businessmen's meeting. The lady who took her, Mrs. Margaret Todd was Ruth's boss at Carson Pirie Scott in Urbana. The Todd's had been very churchy people and were very active in the Christian church in Villa Grove. They had held every office in the church and taught Sunday school. However, they had been visited a year or so before by Gus and Juanita Millot, some of their very well-to-do relatives from Dayton, Ohio. These relatives were drinkers and very worldly. They had definitely not been interested in church before this time. They came to Villa Grove just to tell the Todd's about their exciting new life in Christ.

Later, the Millots' called from Dayton to ask the Todd's if they would like to go to Israel with them to visit the Holy Land. Paul and Margaret along with their fifteen-year old daughter Debbie went for the tour and their lives were radically changed by the power of God while they were in Israel. Margaret realized when she was standing by the Eastern gate in Jerusalem that she did not really have a personal relationship with Jesus. The guide told them that when Jesus returned to the earth, there would be an earthquake and the earth would split, probably just about where they were standing. She called on the name of the Lord and was born-again!

The Todd's were still not too sure about the Pentecostal experience that Gus and Juanita and others on the trip were talking about. However, they stopped in Dayton, Ohio on the way back home to Villa Grove and attended a Full Gospel Businessmen's meeting. At that meeting their fifteen-year old daughter, Debbie, received the baptism in the Holy Spirit, with the evidence of speaking in tongues. It made believers out of them, and Margaret and Paul received this experience soon afterwards.

When they returned to Villa Grove, they shared their testimony about meeting Jesus and this experience with their friends and relatives. Ruth, from our Sunday night Bible study was one of these. The Todd's took people to Full Gospel Business Meetings to receive from the Lord. At that time there were not very many chapters of the inter-denominational organization, and they had to travel back to Dayton, Ohio. The Todd's soon got in touch with a group of Foursquare Church people from Urbana, IL. Pentecostal churches had been around, we just did not know about them. Most of these churches began during a revival in the early part of the nineteen hundred's and while they loved Jesus and lived holy lives, much legalism and separatism had stifled the revival that brought that former move of the Spirit into being.

I asked Jesus to come into my life during this time. One night in bed, I confessed to Jesus that I was a sinner, and would He please forgive me. That night I had a dream, or vision, of Jesus. The experience was in black and white. The blood of Jesus touched me, as the presence of the Holy Spirit washed over my body. I told the Lord that I would serve Him. I knew He was real, and wisdom said, if God is real, serve Him. Every day, I am so thankful that Jesus is not only my Savior, but He is my best friend.

Also, about that time someone gave me a tract called "The Four Spiritual Laws" that is put out by Campus Crusade's ministry. I had already accepted Christ, but I was amazed to read the simple plan of salvation put in that format, and I thought that every church member as well as every lost person in the world, needed to read it and understand it. Later I learned the story of how Bill Bright, the founder of Campus Crusade, came to put that tract together. He was planning on starting with the fact that everyone has sinned and needs a savior, but the Lord appeared to him in a dream and told him to begin the tract with Law number one: God loves you, and he has a wonderful plan for your life. This is based on John 10:10. Jesus came that we might have life, and that life is an abundant life.

One night, my friend Judy, had asked her pastor from Webber Street Church of Christ to speak to the home group on water baptism. Her pastor was not too interested in Pentecost, but he was a go-getter for the Lord with a local television show and a good-sized congregation. He was willing to come to Tolono to speak to the home group. The group met at our house that night and so Jerry happened to be there. That night, pastor John gave an excellent teaching on the importance of immersion as the method for being water baptized. Well, since Ruth and I had not been saved when we were baptized as children, we were excited about following the Biblical method of water baptism. So, at ten o'clock at night we all traipsed up to Webber Street Church of Christ, and John baptized us in water. I do not recall how many were baptized, but I know he offered to baptize Jerry. Jerry declined because he had not yet made a commitment to the Lord. He did go along though and watch the happenings. This baptism had nothing to do with church membership because the pastor knew we were from various denominations.

One night the elders from Webber Street Church of Christ came to our home meeting, which was at Ruth's folk's house that week. As we got into a circle of prayer, Judy ran into the next room. Ruth followed her, and when they came back into the room, Judy was speaking in tongues. She also prophesied that Jesus loved us. She was the first one of the group in Tolono to receive the Baptism in the Holy Spirit locally.

The Lord was working on Jerry, but he had not made a commitment. He had recently gone on a business trip, and he was convicted about the amount of liquor he had consumed while gone.

Ruth had invited us to go to the Todd's home to hear their testimony first-hand and to learn more about the Baptism in the Holy Spirit. I had the car the night that we were to go to Villa Grove. Jerry worked in Champaign, so I told him that I would pick him up after work, we could get a bite to eat and head straight for the Todd's. He had forgotten about the invitation, and had not really planned on going with us, but since I had the car, it worked out that he went along without too much complaining. Jerry's mom lived in Tolono at that time, so she kept the kids.

When we arrived at the Todd's, Margaret got straight to the point. She had a large Jerusalem Bible on the coffee table, and she opened it up and began by sharing her testimony and teaching on the Baptism of the Holy Spirit from the word of God. Her husband and daughter were there, and they shared their testimonies, too. There was great excitement in those early meetings as everyone loved to tell what the Lord was doing in their lives. I absolutely loved hearing their stories. Jerry sat in a corner and says he tried to not listen and still act polite. However, the Holy Spirit was working on him.

After an hour or so, Margaret said that they were going to a prayer meeting at Kenny and Pauline Todd's house just across town, and she invited us to go with her. I think she saw that we were willing to go. At this prayer meeting were some of their new Foursquare friends. One of the ladies lived in Villa Grove but most were from

Champaign. Jerry says he hesitated, wondering if he should go down the street to the local bar instead. However, he went in with us and he says that when he entered the front door, the Holy Spirit came upon him and he encountered the risen Christ. He has loved the Lord from that time on. He said that he felt his burdens and sins lift from him. We had a wonderful prayer meeting as we stood in a circle and praised the Lord together with all our hearts. I loved it! I had asked the Lord to please not let my walk with Him be boring….and I was finding it a wonderful walk.

The next Sunday Jerry surprised me. For the first time he woke up saying we were all going to church together. We attended the Methodist church that morning as a family. Then that night he wanted to visit a new Assembly of God church on Race Street in Urbana. The Todd's had been attending that church. That night at the church service we sensed the same Spirit that we had experience at the prayer meeting in Kenny and Pauline's house the week before, and we were overjoyed. The following week Bob Schmidgall from Naperville, Illinois was going to be at the church to preach a revival. We went every service, and Jerry went forward and publicly gave his life to Christ. He was water baptized, and Pastor Foth prophesied he would become a fisher of men. At that time the church was very small with most of the people being students at the University of Illinois. Pastor Dick Foth was also getting advanced degrees while pastoring. At that time, Pastor Foth had two little girls and his wife Ruth was pregnant. They lived in the church basement. We had Sunday school in their living room.

OUR LIFESTYLE CHANGES

Urbana Assembly opened their arms to this new move of God, and Pastor Foth was an excellent teacher. We sang choruses, testified, and had a good time. We attended every time the doors were open as well as attending home meetings and any special meetings out of town. We took the boys with us most of the time, and sometimes they stayed at grandma's, but we sought the Lord when we gathered, and the presence of God was manifest.

During this time, people were experiencing similar happenings across the country. At this time Pat Boone's book, A New Song, came out which told of his Pentecostal experience. Since he had been a big singing star his book had great impact. He also starred in the movie made of Cross and the Switchblade. During this time a best seller was a book, They Speak with Other Tongues by John Sherrill, which was an excellent teaching on the history of Pentecost from a denominational churchman's point of view. The book told of the new wave of the Spirit that was beginning to happen. Sherrill was also a writer for Guideposts and a good friend of Normal Vincent Peale. This book explained the moving of God so anyone with an open heart could understand it.

Jerry was hungry for the baptism of the Holy Spirit, too. A couple of weeks after attending the Todd's prayer meeting, and Jerry's conversion, they invited us to attend a FGBMFI (Full Gospel Businessmen's Fellowship International) meeting at the Chase Plaza Hotel in St. Louis. Jerry canceled his pre-Jesus fishing trip plans to go.

Ruth, Jerry and I were to meet the Todd's in St. Louis at the hotel. When we entered the hotel, a short Dutchman from Africa, met us and said his name was Robert Thom and that he cast out devils. He invited us to his room for a prayer meeting. He must have sensed that we still needed some deliverance. In the weeks ahead Robert Thom came to Champaign and ministered to us in different homes and at Full Gospel meetings. He said God had sent him to the United States, and his wife and family did not mind him being here.

There were many different speakers at that first convention we attended in St. Louis. Most had dynamite testimonies of the changing power of God, and they always stressed the power of God to do miracles. We heard Cash Amburgy, who was a businessman from Dayton Ohio. He jumped all over the place when he preached. Some people liked the quiet teachers, and some of us liked the rowdy passionate speakers. I liked them all! Pauline Todd's daughter Terri sang at some of the conventions. She was only thirteen, so this was a treat. At that first convention, I went forward to every altar call for the baptism in the Holy Spirit.

Wendell Wallace was one of the speakers who gave an altar call. Many went forward and received. He called me up on stage, explained the baptism, and I let him down. I just could not receive. He was embarrassed and so was I.

After Cash Amburgy spoke he challenged everyone to run to the prayer room next door if they wanted the baptism in the Holy Spirit. Well, Jerry and I meandered out the door after everyone else ran. We experienced a real miracle! We entered the room and no one else was in it. We sat in the back row. Dr. AG Dornfelt, a Spirit-filled Lutheran pastor from St. Charles, was going to lead the prayer meeting. He came into the room after us, and he grabbed us by the shoulders, asked us if we wanted the Holy Spirit, and ushered us up front to the row of chairs. He explained the Baptism of the Holy Spirit in the scriptures, laid hands on everyone, and most received, including Jerry. He was very blessed! The miracle was that those running out the door in front of us came to the prayer room after us. We still wonder how that miracle took place.

Some ladies told me that if I would lengthen my skirt and quit bleaching my hair that I would get "it." As I looked around the crowd, I noticed that they were the only ones there with no make-up and it did not stop the other people from receiving. I had repented and repented of every sin that I could think of. My problem was faith. Judy and Jerry had seen a light when they received. I did not feel what I thought I should feel or have any other manifestations. At the last altar call, I knelt between two Catholic nuns. They both received as hands were laid on them. I had one word. GLEEK. That could not be the Holy Spirit, I reasoned.

MY EXPERIENCE

Jerry, Ruth, and I went for lunch and I felt like I was drunk, much like on the day of Pentecost written about in the book of Acts. I thought everything was beautiful, including the restaurant. Jerry and Ruth insisted we leave because it was filthy. I did not notice, I was so happy, as they led me to another restaurant. Now I know that I received the Baptism, because I did speak in tongues, but the devil convinced me otherwise on the way home. Besides, my new-Christian non-experienced husband and friend said it probably wasn't the baptism since I only got one word. They both had powerful supernatural experiences when they received the baptism in the Holy Spirit. A major truth to remember is that the word of God is what we determine our experience on, not feelings and not what other people experience. I spoke in tongues, I asked for the Holy Spirit, and Jesus baptized me during that meeting. Even if I did only speak one word. Each person must receive the baptism in the Holy Spirit like everything else in the Bible and in God's kingdom. By faith.

My life changed radically as I gave my life to Jesus. When we got home from St. Louis, and I began to pray in my private time with the Lord, I immediately prayed fluently in tongues. I still had doubts. Maybe it was just me. Many days later, I found myself praying in tongues along with the television set's Beverly Hillbillies theme song which was playing in the background. I cried out to the Lord for confirmation that this was truly His Spirit giving me the utterance, and as I opened my Bible it fell open to Luke 11:9-13. This verse says that if we, being evil, know how to give good gifts to our children, how much more will the Father give the Holy Spirit to them that ask. I never doubted that I had received the Holy Spirit again. I had asked Jesus for the baptism in the Holy Spirit, and His word is true. Also, at that same time, He gave me a vision of a house we would live in. I did not recognize the house until later after we had moved into it.

Jerry and I were so excited about the Lord and His kingdom. We both devoured the Bible and loved to hear the word preached and taught. We also loved Pentecostal meetings of any kind. At every home meeting we were praying for someone new to receive the baptism in the Holy Spirit. We were beginning to move in the gifts of the Spirit. We loved the teachings on faith and devoured teaching books by Kenneth Hagin, Oral Roberts and others. Many were written very simply, making it easy to grasp the concepts that were taught. Our hearts were open and hungry for Jesus.

We all witnessed at every opportunity about how the Lord was real to us. The home meetings grew and multiplied. There were many people who were getting interested in the Lord, but who still were not willing to come into a Pentecostal meeting. We were hearing of their testimonies. Some of our old pre-Christian friends from Champaign had started attending church and were seeking a real relationship with Jesus. The radical change that Jesus made was seen in people's lives and our testimonies all had an impact.

THE OUTPOURING EXPANDS

When Jerry and I attended that first FBMFI convention in St. Louis, Gus and Juanita Millot from Dayton, told him he should go back to Champaign-Urbana and begin a chapter there. Now here we were, brand new believers and she expected Jerry to lead a Christian group! He laughed at the thought, but he said he would go home and pray about it for a week. Each night we would read and pray before going to sleep. The last night of his commitment, Jerry prayed, and the Lord gave him a vision. The Lord appeared as the Ancient of Days and showed him the Bible and said not to fear the face of men.

Through Margaret Todd, we were put in touch with several older men who were in denominational churches in Champaign but had received the baptism in the Holy Spirit. I remember Gene Ziegler, Keith Shepherd, Chuck Tiecher and several others who were on our board of directors. In the very late sixties and early seventies, our Champaign-Urbana Chapter was one of the very first chapters. The Chicago chapter may have been the only other one in Illinois at that time. People like David DuPlessie, Nicky Cruz, and many other Christian leaders came to speak.

At later St. Louis convention's I remember hearing Kenneth Copeland speak in the youth meeting at one convention. He was just getting started. Some of the keynote speakers were Kenneth Hagin, Katheryn Kuhlman, Oral Roberts, Derrick Prince and others. We saw wonderful miracles take place.

Jerry and the other officers also put together a convention in one of the large hotels in Champaign, and many people from the area came to it. I remember a single lady, Roxanne Brant, who taught and ministered some powerful truths. She was billed as a debutante from New York. She was a beautiful and anointed speaker. Many revelations we had were confirmed through her ministry. She had a vision of some devastation to come. Jerry had a vision of floods and fires across America. Some things do not happen immediately, we have come to realize. We need to hold on to the prophetic and keep them in our hearts.

David Wilkerson came to Champaign, and we helped with his crusade. That was such a blessing after all his book had meant to us. Through the years we have had a special kindred spirit to those who have a ministry to the streets. It was our calling for many years.

We, also, had weird teaching by some teachers who came to minister, but the Lord seemed to let us know what was true. I remember one man said he could look at people's feet and tell them spiritual things to come. That sounded too much like palm reading to me. I thank the Lord that we had an early knowledge of the word. His grace enables us to read and understand the Bible. I remember pre-conversion days when I tried to read the Bible and gave up after a paragraph or two. The Bible says the non-spiritual man does not understand the things of God.

I also remember some young men who were part of a campus group who got off base. The leaders were very controlling, almost like a cult. Later teaching on spiritual abuse came out, but at that time many people got sucked in because some of the leaders were popular athletes from

Charismatic Renewal

the University. I heard that they knocked over showcases in a Catholic bookstore and did other destructive actions in their misplaced zeal. They ended up in trouble for physically abusing a child when disciplining him. We later ministered to a couple who had some real emotional damage from being a part of the group. During that time I asked the Lord why people followed teachers who so obviously off base. The Lord spoke to my heart that many are not contented with the quiet, peaceful life of true Christianity, and so they are looking for something different than the simple gospel message.

There were other people who got involved in Manifested Sons doctrine, which said that Christians would never die. There was a man who came to Danville, several years later when we were at Westcove who was a real nut. A pastor in Danville invited him in to hold meetings at his church and then turned the church over to him. Quite a few people went to the meetings and then stayed at the church. This guy dressed like a Catholic Priest, wore a Jewish cap, and said his hands bled where the nail prints were in Jesus hands. It is called stigmata, and this was his big promotion. He ended up deceiving the previous pastor's wife, and that pastor came to Jerry for counsel. We formed a circle and prayed for the Lord to please intervene. That very night there was a car wreck and the deceiver was killed. It put the fear of God in us. To be honest, the fear of God has always been in us enough to not want to play with the things of God.

Corrie Ten Boom came to Champaign and at about eighty years of age, she passionately told about her life during the Nazi invasion of her homeland and of how Jesus was so real to her during that time. She called herself a cheerleader for Jesus. She was a very good Bible teacher, and she ministered powerfully to the Charismatic community.

Many pastors were not too excited about this interdenominational or trans-denominational move of the Holy Spirit. I praise the Lord that Urbana Assembly accepted us and the move of God that was happening. I've heard it said that people who experienced the last move of God often are most resistant to the next move of God. I pray that will never be true in my life. I want to be ready when Jesus comes back. Most of the Jews in Jesus time missed their Messiah because He did not come the way they expected. We must stay close to the Lord and in His word so that we love the truth more than the world or our traditions. We must recognize what the Spirit is saying to the church. Also, we need to recognize what the Spirit is doing in the world. The Pharisees in Jesus day could not receive a Messiah who was a common carpenter's son, who spit in the dirt to heal a blind man on the Sabbath, and who hung out with sinners. Preconceived ideas can make us miss God's best.

Also, at this same time the Youth for Christ organization was being used to reach the teenagers in Champaign. They, too, were having all night prayer meetings and seeing God move in their midst. Many were coming to know the Lord. They found that the more commitment to Christ they called for, the more the teens dedicated their lives to Christ. The leaders cut back on the number of social outreaches as they found that they often hindered the kid's commitment to God.

The congregation at Urbana Assembly was mostly college students to begin with, but people of all ages were beginning to come to the church. One of the students was Byron Klause who at that time was in the school of agriculture. He is now in Springfield as President of the Assemblies of God Seminary. I occasionally see other Assembly of God leaders who went through the Assembly in Urbana during that time. We recently

Charismatic Renewal

attended the Urbana Assembly for a few months, before coming to pastor in Paris, and it was exciting to see the church with over a thousand members. However, the most exciting part is that there are people from all over the world attending from practically every nation of the world. Most are there because of the University of Illinois. I think Pastor Grogan said there are over fifty ethnic groups represented. Think of the potential they have for the gospel as they return their countries after they finish their education.

One service that I especially remember attending as a new believer was an evening service. Brad and Charles had been misbehaving so I took them our into the foyer to give them a talking to. As you can imagine I was not in a real spiritual mood. When I walked back into the sanctuary the people were all praying around the altar. As I looked, I could see sparkles all over in the air, and the Lord impressed me that it was the Shekinah glory of the Lord in the room. It was certainly not emotionalism that manifested that miracle, but God's great mercy.

PREACHING THE GOSPEL PUBLICALLY

About this same time, we decided that we needed to tell others about the Lord and not just go to meetings and be blessed for ourselves. One of the speakers at FGBMFI had prophesied over Jerry that he was to preach. That same night the Lord also spoke to Jerry and said, "Minister me to my people."

At this time the revival movement had really begun to spread around the country. There were FGBMFI chapters in many of the larger towns, and people everywhere were having meetings in their homes, and other public places. We were daily meeting house to house and talking about the things of God. I had a burden for Rossville, my hometown, so we put up flyers and put an ad in the paper, saying, "God is not Dead, Come Hear!" We rented the town hall and took along the Todd's and a few others to share their testimonies. They shared their testimonies and Jerry ended with a clear, short simple message on salvation and the Baptism of the Holy Spirit. Twelve were saved that night and later received the Baptism. My sister, Judy Rayfield and a good friend Carolyn Barragree and her husband Dennis were among those first converts. They have their own stories to tell of spiritual revival in that area as the years have passed. God is faithful, and He is the one who gives the increase.

We continued to have meetings in that area.

Eventually, several years later, a full-gospel church was established by a friend from high school and his wife, Jim and Temple Lloyd. They have a powerful testimony also. They became Christians after their marriage had broken up. She was an Episcopalian and he had fallen into sin. God saved them, healed their marriage, and they went to Rhema Bible School in Tulsa. He is a leader in the Charismatic Fellowship that their church is a part of today. Many of my family are Christians today and actively serving the Lord from that area. I want to mention that people were delivered from the deception of homosexuality which was very hush-hush back then.

We also went to Villa Grove, Farmers City, and other small towns preaching the gospel in the same manner. Several came to Urbana Assembly as they received the baptism and were not comfortable in their old churches anymore. A group had started a church in Tolono, but it folded, and one night they knocked on our door and asked if we wanted to take it over. We prayed about it, but we did not feel like it was what the Lord wanted for us. We were comfortable with being evangelists.

We did not feel qualified at that time to pastor, and we loved the church in Urbana which was still relatively small. We would have felt guilty leaving it. We also loved the home groups and fellowship we were having in our home meetings. Often the speakers at FGBMFI would want to speak other places when they came to town. Sometimes we could get them a church, but often we had them into home meetings.

One night I was afraid we would not have enough people come to the home meeting, because we were having one of the speakers who was going to speak at the Full Gospel Businessmen meeting. Our Bible study met in various houses and did not really have a regular teacher or leader, we just read and prayed, expecting the Holy Spirit to come and bless us. I decided to fast that day. It was the first fast that I remember, and it was not a long one, just until the meeting that night. The meeting was to be in our basement. That night people just streamed into the house, and we had a basement full of people. I remember some Catholic nuns being there that night among other people I did not know at all. It was a supernatural gathering.

One couple who was a part of our home group was a young Methodist minister and his wife, Charles and Judy, from Sadorus, Illinois. His wife told of a supernatural angelic visitor she had from childhood. Even in our inexperience, we knew that it was demonic. She was open to deliverance, so the group prayed, and she did not experience any more visitations.

They preached healing and the other things they were learning but eventually left the Methodist Church. They later were pastors of a large Charismatic church in northern Indiana. The church was a spin off from Gerald Derstine's ministry. Gerald Derstine was a Mennonite minister who had great influence in the Charismatic renewal. He has the Christian Retreat Center in Bradenton, Florida and has written many teaching books. We met him through Charles and Judy, and later our family visited the Center one year on vacation. Jason, Rachel and Sarah were still at home and went with us. They had a ball as they met other kids their age around the pool. Reba Rambo and her husband ministered while we were there. Charles' parents and other family members were all involved in the move of God and were great supporters of Full Gospel Businessmen.

In the early seventies we had an opportunity to have fellowship and communion with some Catholic priests we met through the Full Gospel meetings. During that time frame they began a full-gospel Catholic Church in the old Foursquare building in Urbana. For several years, they had a ministry to Catholics in Urbana. Many people in the Charismatic renewal were Catholics.

One of my best friends from childhood, Gayle Bowman, was Catholic and Gayle had moved to North Little Rock after high school. After I witnessed to her she never contacted me when she came home on vacation. She would play golf with my mom. But, several years later, she called and said she had gone to a Billy Graham meeting and accepted Christ and joined a Baptist Church. Then later, she stopped by our house on vacation and said the whole church had gone Charismatic, and she was involved in a cell group.

I remember the Catholics used wine for their communion. Many of the people were used to taking wine at communion. One time we drove through a liquor store to buy some to take to Rossville. I would never do that today! While many Charismatic's have felt free to drink wine, our early Methodist background and Assemblies affiliation has kept us from ever drinking beyond these communion experiences.

Many of the Lutheran's used wine in communion. Later when we attended Christian Outreach Center in Missouri most of the people had Lutheran backgrounds. We were shocked to see those we considered to be on-fire Christians drinking beer. Our boys were really upset over it. I remember, Jamie Buckingham, a popular Christian writer during that time, writing an article in Charisma magazine, saying that while he saw the freedom in Christ to do so, he repented of drinking socially and was quitting because of the stumbling block it was to others. My feeling is that we want to be a clear witness to

Charismatic Renewal

our children and grandchildren. Besides I would rather be drunk in the Spirit than wine any day! The Bible says be ye not drunk with wine, but be ye filled with the Holy Ghost.

I want to mention Bill Lowery, because he did have an influence on us, and he also had a great impact in spreading the gospel during the late sixties and early seventies in our entire area. Bill and Sarah had grown up in a small town outside of Champaign, gotten radically saved under Rev. Eddie Cunningham's ministry. Bill had grown up in the Methodist church and was brought into the Baptism of the Holy Spirit through Rev. Cunningham who was Assemblies of God minister. Bill then became an evangelist.

Bill wanted to have a tent meeting in Tolono, and he knew us from FGBMFI, so he asked us to help. We were excited to do so. At that time Bill was into what we called "holiness." He wore long sleeved white shirts and suits in the heat of the summer. No tie, no holiness, was his motto! He played a great guitar and sang wonderful choruses as well as preached good sermons. He was able to have some wonderful meetings. Irene Garabrant, the Methodist minister's wife attended the tent meeting one night. By this time we had left the Methodist church and joined Urbana Assembly. However, many of the Methodists visited the Assemblies, and no one was upset about it.

That night Mrs. Garabrant got touched by the Holy Spirit and began to run around the tent praising the Lord. At just that time Jim and Bill came by to see what was happening. They saw their pastor's wife have a supernatural experience, and it made believers out of them concerning Pentecost. Irene was a very quiet sophisticated woman, but that night she was running around the tent shouting praises to Jesus. Each one of these people has their own stories and is serving the Lord today. The Garabrant's continued to minister in Methodist Churches through the years. In fact, years later, he performed the wedding ceremony for our son's wedding when Charles and Brook were married at the Methodist Church in Sidell.

One special testimony from Bill Lowery's tent meeting in Tolono was the salvation of Bud Harris. After pitching the tent, we drove down the alley behind the tavern next to the tent and Bud Harris was mowing their yard. He was "the" town drunk, and I mentioned to Bill and Jerry that it would be great to see Bud saved. Others with me kind of chuckled. That night, some of Bud's six kids came to the meeting. Their uncle and aunt had been a part of our home meetings. Jackie and Richard Harris attended the Curtis Avenue Church of God in Champaign and they had been a help in our early understanding of Pentecost. Even though Bud was the town drunk, his mother was a Methodist, and he was from a good family. Anyway, Bud staggered into the meeting late to see his kids, and we encouraged him to come the following night.

We assured him that he could wear anything and that clothes did not matter. He came the next night, and when Bill gave an appeal for prayer requests at the beginning of the meeting, Bud walked through the chairs and said he wanted to get saved! From that day forward, Bud was one of our best friends and a faithful supporter of every outreach that we had or that Bill had in the area. He shared his testimony with everyone, everywhere, and only heaven will tell how many he led to the Lord. When he went to be with the Lord at age fifty, it took hours for everyone to get into the visitation. His children and family are serving the Lord today in the Church of God.

Charismatic Renewal

One thing happened that I thought was humorous. The day after Bud got saved in the tent meeting, he came to our house to see Bill and Jerry. I still remember he had on a flowered shirt and striped shorts and was smoking a cigarette. Bill did not say a word about how he was dressed, but we had a little laugh about it, since Bill at that time was convinced he needed to wear a suit no matter how hot it was.

Bill Lowery later became a part of the Jesus Movement and changed his method of dress and ministry. Several years later when we had moved to Danville, Bill came back into the area after spending several years in Florida and in the Northern part of Illinois with the tent. He preached in various towns in Central Illinois. At one large meeting in Urbana, he had a star from Nashville and Little Richard. He had an entourage of people who traveled with him and many were young people who witnessed on the streets before the meeting. He was a true part of the Jesus Movement! They had several semis to pack their gear, and they also traveled to Europe and began churches that are still in existence today. It was hands-on discipleship and Christian community for those who traveled with him. My son Charles, who was about eight at the time, loved Bill and I remember him saying when he grew up, he wanted to be a hippie like Bill and preach about Jesus.

Bill's brother Doug Lowery now pastors a large church in Decatur and is one of our Presbyters for the Illinois District of the Assemblies of God. He started out helping Bill. The one weakness of Bill was that he was anti-denominational, and although his points had truth to them, it often did not make for friendship with the established church. Churches, like people are not perfect, but Jesus still calls us to love the church as well as one another, and His plan is to work through the local church.

Bill preached that all true believers in an area are the true church. That the church is a matter of locality and consists of people who have truly given their lives to Jesus, not denominational buildings which are divisive. Today, he has fallen out of church, and we pray for him

Our kids were shuffled around way too much during those years, and I often wonder what the church world looked like through their eyes. Later when Charles was a teen-ager, he came home after visiting a church with a friend, and he was so surprised that no one raised their hands when they worshipped. Years later our youngest daughter was radically changed in the Brownsville revival in Florida. When we visited a Church of God in Huntsville, a lady's hand quivered as she praised the Lord. Sarah asked if she had been to Brownsville. I laughed as I told her that people had praised the Lord like that many, many places, not just Brownsville. Each generation needs to live in the moving of the Spirit. I am glad to see freshness of the Spirit springing up in many places where Jesus' presence is coveted above all else.

Charismatic Renewal

TAKING JESUS TO THE SUBURBS

We decided to move from Tolono to a house in Champaign. We had thought we would build in Tolono, but after getting saved, we did not want to take the time. We had already sold our old house and were renting. Since we were involved in the church in Urbana and FGBMFI, we decided to move back to Champaign. We thought about Bible school, but I had four children now, and we just did not have the faith or unction to make that move. We really thought the Lord was coming back any minute. I am not going to apologize or evaluate everything we did back then with the knowledge that I have now. We, like all followers of Jesus have repented, and been thankful always for God's grace. Our mistakes have not been intentional, but out of ignorance of God's ways. I just praise the Lord that the Lord has blessed us and taken care of our family over the years.

At that time we had four boys. In 1970, I had Jason, who was my first baby after conversion, and I felt so blessed to have another baby. The women at Urbana Assembly had a shower for me. I remember going down to the basement and there was a city road sign that said Leroy which was Jason's middle name. One of the students had gotten it??? I still wonder about that one.

I moved in next door to Connie who was chairman of Christian Women's Club. She became a dear friend, and I became book chairman for that group. She invited me to a Bible study on Colossians. The whole Bible study ended up receiving the baptism in the Holy Ghost. Connie went to a large Baptist church in Mahomet, and she struggled with my testimony for some time. One day she took me witnessing, and we shared the four spiritual laws with the whole neighborhood. She was bold, and she was a very dedicated wife and mother. One day after reading <u>They Speak with Other Tongues</u> by John Sherrill, she called me and asked me to pray with her. I was glad my friend Judy from Tolono was visiting and could go with me. Connie was even more on fire for the Lord after she received the baptism in the Holy Spirit. Later on she and I co-hosted a Charismatic Women's Outreach at one of the hotels, and we had a great turn out of ladies come to the meeting, and they experienced the moving of the Holy Spirit. It was one of the first full-gospel, inter-denominational ladies meetings in that area. Later Women Aglow was started.

We had meetings in our home, and many of the ladies from Christian Women's Club came. I remember one of the speakers from FGBMFI, who was from some prominent family, saying that there were women from a lot of different social backgrounds represented. I hadn't noticed until he said something. The moving of the Holy Spirit drew us all together as one.

There were home meetings and Bible studies springing up in little towns all around Champaign, and people were receiving the baptism in the Holy Spirit. The Holy Spirit was drawing people together.

I was praying one day when the Lord spoke to me the words "New Castle, Indiana." It was so real, that I got out a map and looked it up. The next day, we received an invitation to a convention that a new Full Gospel chapter was holding in New Castle, Indiana. I was so excited that I called everyone I knew. A large group of us went over to it and while we were not speakers, we all witnessed around the tables, etc. We were blessed by being there, too. Later we lived in New Castle and tried to pioneer a church. We did not succeed, and the enemy won that round.

But going back to when we lived in Champaign, I remember driving by the housing projects, and the Lord spoke to my heart that we would someday minister to the poor. I thought, well everyone cries poor, and did not really think too much about it until later when we spent twenty years in City Mission work as home missionaries ministering to the homeless.

We only spent a year in Champaign because Jerry had lost his job, and he got a new one in Danville. The company he worked for on campus closed its doors. It was a tough year financially for us, but also it was a year of spiritual growth. We kept busy, but there was very little income coming in. I put a beauty shop in the basement. We learned to trust God, and we were also humbled in many ways. We had bought a small school bus and painted it to use for evangelism. We took the puppets and did a few outreaches in the surrounding area towns. We also picked up kids for the Vacation Bible School at Urbana Assembly, and I won a concordance as a prize for bringing the most people. We were shocked to win a prize, and we used that concordance for many years.

DANVILLE: A NEW AREA OF OUTREACH

Moving to Danville was a whole new area spiritually. Danville was Jerry's hometown, and it was where he grew up. We had made friends with a man who had been pastor of the Methodist church on Fairchild Street in Danville. We had ministered in his church when we were holding meetings before. A group from the Teen Challenge in Indianapolis came to his church, and they stayed at our house part of the time they were there. I can't really remember the details of how that all took place, but we believed the Lord was leading us to go to Bill's church when we moved to Danville and help as we could. Things went well until we had an outreach meeting at the local YMCA and advertised that God would do miracles. A man received his sight in that meeting. Suddenly we began to feel the cold shoulder at the Methodist church. However, Jerry's mom went to that church for many years, and in the late eighties, when the church closed, they donated a large amount of money to the local rescue mission that we founded. We then went to the Danville Assembly of God, and we heard they were a little upset that we had not gone directly to that church. It seemed relatively easy for us to get into trouble without trying.

We moved to a house on Robinson Street, and it was a totally different neighborhood than the neighborhood in Champaign. However, it was a mission field. Four teen-agers from the neighborhood came to the door as we were moving in and said that they had seen our Christian bumper stickers. We asked if they had received the Holy Ghost since they believed, and they said no. We prayed, and they all received the baptism of the Holy Spirit before we even had the furniture in. Greg, our oldest son was thirteen at the time, and the kids felt quite at home. They spent many evenings at our house talking about the Lord, and while we have lost track of most of them, I know one girl ended up in a singing group, and they sang in some of our tent meetings. I ran into another guy, years later when visiting Urbana Assembly. The Lord has holding power. Many of these kids were from very fragile or broken families.

We started going to Danville Assembly of God, and we really enjoyed the teaching and the music. We met a young Lutheran couple, Linda and Ron, who attended there, and we became friends. They in turn invited us to meet some friends of theirs from work who were interested in the Holy Spirit. We met with a group of several couples, and they were hungry for the Holy Spirit. Don and Dorothy, Methodists, had been exposed to Pentecostals through his family in Detroit. They were a few years older and the leading couple in the group. Later this home group invited a minister down from Detroit, and they started the Rock Church. In those early meetings, we taught on the baptism in the Holy Spirit, and several of them received. It was a fun time in the Lord. Their church had a great influence during the following years. We left Danville to do tent evangelism before the church began, and the Hanson's, one of the leading couples, visited us when we were in New Castle to update us on what all was happening.

We had other meetings in our home with people from Danville we had met through FGBMFI. The neighborhood kids also came. I had a couple of women's outreaches in my home and Connie came over from Champaign and shared her testimony and scripture. We saw good results from those meetings of fifteen to twenty women.

God was bringing new people into the church daily, just like in the book of Acts. We attended home meetings in Rossville, my hometown, on a pretty regular basis. I remember my sister-in-law saying, "Maybe Jerry will be the next Billy Graham." The Lord immediately spoke to my heart and said, "No, there will be a lot of Jerry Jones." That is exactly what was happening in this move of God. Many ordinary people were preaching the gospel with no intentions of a huge ministry. We just wanted everyone to know Jesus and have eternal life. We wanted them to learn how to move in the gifts of the Spirit like in the book of Acts and to experience God's presence.

In Danville Jerry hated working at the factory he was in. In Champaign, even though he only had his electronics training from the service, he had worked in research as a technician with engineering opportunities. Right after we became Christians and still lived in Tolono, the company Jerry worked for sent him to Italy a couple of times on an assignment. On the second trip it was possible for me to go along, and I was so excited. My mother was willing to take care of the kids so I could go. We prayed that God would use us while we were there.

We visited a little Assembly of God Church way up in the hills when we arrived in Naples. The pastor told us that Catholics there were persecuted if they converted and left their church, and that often it was dangerous. We could see that Catholicism was much different in Italy than it was in the states.

While in Italy, we visited a church on one of the military bases, and it opened some wonderful doors for us. We were invited to one of the missionary's home. We shared to their entire Nazarene group about the baptism in the Holy Spirit. Being overseas they didn't seem to care about church doctrine, they were just hungry. The women took me all over the area and showed me the sights while Jerry worked, and I had a wonderful time. We were also invited to the home of the Commander of the Mediterranean Fleet for dinner. The wanted us to share all our testimony and what the Lord was doing through FGBMFI. Later when we were back in the states, he called us and said that they had received the baptism in the Spirit. I still am amazed at that open door.

While in Danville, the scripture about the rich young ruler plagued me. Did houses mean more to me than the gospel??? Not that we were rich by any means. We always lived paycheck to paycheck. In fact, one of the miracles of our walk with Jesus is that we have never had a serious financial problem that the Lord has not seen us through. Many times through the years, we have really been nip and tuck. I often laughed and said we were not poor, just broke a lot. I am sure my older children remember growing up without extras. Jerry had a radio program during that time, but we could not tell what results we were getting. We gave up because we could not afford it on our paycheck. At that time, we tried to "live by faith" but had trouble pressing through those tough spots.

One day as I was praying about Jerry's job, the Lord spoke to me that I would minister to women. It was out of the blue, and I knew that God had spoken to me. Also, I already enjoyed having women gather together so it was just a confirmation. But it was wonderful to hear the Holy Spirit speak to my heart.

Merlyn Carothers wrote a popular book <u>Prison to Praise</u> about praising the Lord in all circumstances that was a best seller. We had met Merlyn through FGBMFI. He was a Methodist minister and ministered close to Danville in Ambia and Locust Grove, Indiana. He asked Jerry to fill his pulpits during this time. His daughter and many others responded to the altar call when we were there. Merlyn had planted and watered, and we had the blessing to see the response. Merlyn spurred revival in that area, and I marvel at God's grace to send a man like Merlyn to that area. We appreciated knowing him. I remember he gave Jerry a set of commentaries that later Jerry in turn passed on to one of his students at COC. I kind of wish we had kept them!

We felt the Lord was leading us to do tent evangelism. Jerry was a good teacher and preacher. We read enough books and listened to enough teachings; we should have been able to preach! However, discipleship is about a whole lot more than preaching. We did not feel confident enough to think about being pastors. However, even then Jerry felt like it someday it would be his calling, and we did love church! The Lord spoke to Jerry and said, "Do not get caught up in a cause." We passed up several chances to sell Amway during the years, and even though we have been active advocates for the unborn, and worked with the homeless, we have tried to stay focused on evangelism and discipleship as our main ministry focus.

I remember that we had a meeting at Mann's Chapel, a little antique church outside of my hometown of Rossville, and quite a few family members and people from Indiana came. Several who were touched in that revival went on to spread the gospel in their home areas. We did get some persecution, but mostly just crazy things, like one man said Jerry had people kissing his feet! The only thing we could figure was he had never seen people on their knees at an altar before. I still love that little church. Years before when the ladies in the historical society decided to clear out the pigeon dung and make it a landmark, the Methodist youth group did the scooping and our picture was in the paper. Today, my family members are buried in the cemetery surrounding the church.

Anyway, just as we had sold the house in Danville and bought the ministry tent and camper, I found out that I was pregnant again. We were too far into it to have second thoughts. We had sold or given away all the furniture and cut all ties. So, we and the four boys packed into the camper and took off, preaching the gospel. The Lord said that his children would never beg for bread and we didn't, but it was a scary time for me. The kids loved it. My parents, I am sure had bouts of anxiety, but they were gracious, considering at that time they were not Christians. I remember mom saying someone stopped her on the street and said, "Do you know that Jerry and Linda speak in tongues?" Mom said her response was, "Well, it must be in the Bible." God is good! Before we took off, the pastor at First Assembly encouraged Jerry to start his Berean Courses so he could get his ministry license, and he began and finished them during this time. Later we both finished BA degrees in theology through correspondence courses, and I took Berean courses to get licensed with the Assemblies. But that was much later.

SPIRITUAL WARFARE

We preached with the tent in several places through the summer including Hoopeston where some of my relatives were able to come. When fall came, we were keenly aware that the baby was due in November. We had a tent meeting in New Castle, Indiana and had an opportunity to begin a church. We gladly took it as an open door. Jerry also got a job with a local Christian businessman that we had met through Full Gospel.

During this time, we had some real attacks from Satan. Now the Lord was beginning to show us that we had to learn how to fight spiritual battles. Rachel was born in New Castle. At a time when I could have been overjoyed at finally having a baby girl, the battle took the edge off the joy. However, her name means "little lamb," and she has been a blessing to us throughout the years with her sweet spirit and gentle ways.

When we left New Castle several months later for Indianapolis. I learned the lesson of letting things go and forgiving those who would despitefully use you. We lacked discernment in the people we were working with. Later we found out that we were not the first victims or ministers who had been attacked in the same way. We saw people ministered to during that short time, but it was a hard time for our little family. I know that there is not a minister of the gospel who does not go through some fire. While much comes on us through our own ignorance, some comes on us because Satan really does want to kill steal and destroy the children of God. We ran from the battle, and in retrospect, it is a time I think we missed God's best because of it.

INDIANAPOLIS

Jerry got a job in Indianapolis. With five children, we were blessed to find a nice four-bedroom apartment. It was another year of financial stretching, and some fiery attacks of the enemy. I went through a time of real emotional testing because of leaving New Castle and the problems we had faced there. The Lord spoke to me when I cried out to him. The Holy Spirit said the enemy had been defeated at the cross. I had to rest in that victory by faith. I knew that I had to forgive and guard my thoughts to maintain a sound mind. God was faithful, and he strengthened me though it all, and the bad memories finally left.

When in Indianapolis, a friend from Rossville came to visit, and she told me about a new organization called Women Aglow that was much like FGBMFI only it was for women. As I prayed about it I knew the Lord wanted me to start a chapter in Indianapolis. Some ladies joined with me and helped me organize a meeting. We met at a local country club and had a good turn out from the beginning. I remember one Pentecostal lady got excited and upset a glass of water, and my officers were upset at the public display of emotion. I reprimanded them and said people get excited at ball games, how much more should we be excited about the Lord? They all got excited as time went on.

Charles and Frances Hunter came to minister, and we decided to have it at one of the large Methodist churches where one of the Aglow officers attended. People were lying all over the floor as the power of God fell and many were healed during that meeting. It was one of the most powerful Pentecostal meetings I ever attended.

Jerry had a radio program on local radio in Indianapolis that included testimonies. Television, channel 40, Lester Sumrall's station really helped spread the charismatic renewal in the area, and we were on to advertise the newly formed Aglow.

Cindy, one of the officers of Aglow was part of a home meeting we attended at Dick and Peg's house. Dick was an International Director for FGBMFI, and he and Peg were friends of ours. One night in the middle of the night Dick called and said that Cindy's mother, two sisters, and a young nephew had been killed in a house fire. They were our friends from attending his home meeting, and they already had a sad story. The two sisters had Huntington's disease and both of their husbands had left them because they could not take seeing their wives go downhill. Their mother's husband, who was not the girl's dad, had left because he did not want the responsibility. They were beautiful ladies and had wonderful conversion experiences. Hazel, the mother, especially was a very gracious woman, and she had been so happy at the changes that Jesus had made in her daughter's lives. They had received Christ and became holy young women. Even though they were losing some muscle control, their spirits were sweet, and they were passionate about Jesus. We were all so shocked at their deaths. Cindy and her brother were spared this disease, and continued to serve Jesus, trusting in his eternal plan.

However, all of us were like Abraham. We were looking for the city whose founder and maker is God. There is a New Jerusalem and there will be a new heaven and earth where righteousness dwells. Until then, our best way to win in spiritual warfare is to keep close to Jesus in prayer, live holy, and do not give the devil any footholds by staying out of fellowship with the saints. Christ will build his church, and He is coming back soon to gather those who are eagerly waiting for his return.

While we were in Indianapolis, Bill Lowery's ministry came to town and had a huge tent meeting. By then the entourage consisted of quite a few more semi-trailers full of gear, campers, and numerous members who had joined with the ministry. Bill was overseas and another minister was in charge of the Indianapolis meetings. I hosted a big luncheon for all of the ladies at the clubhouse in our apartment complex, and we invited other women to join us. A lot of people came into the kingdom through their outreach. People heard a message of commitment to Jesus that was different than just joining a church. Our friends, Dick and Peggy thought about going with them, and I am glad they didn't. Jesus said to some of those who believed in Him to sell all and follow him, but that doesn't mean we all leave home to follow Him.

Also, during my time in Indianapolis, I made friends with Jo, a lady whose husband was a state representative, and he also spoke at a lot of Full Gospel meetings. Jo spoke at Aglow, and she was a kindred spirit. They attended a "Faith" church that met in a hotel under Pastor Hobart Freeman. We visited once, but the ladies wore head coverings, and while I loved the teaching, we believed the Lord wanted us in the Assemblies.

Anyway, I loved Jo's zeal for Jesus, and I rode to Terre Haute with her one day when she was invited to speak at a meeting. During the meeting a terrible ice and snowstorm hit and the lady in charge of the meeting wanted us to stay all night. Jo said, by FAITH, we would make it home, and I agreed with her. We rode home over ice and saw many cars in the ditch. When I got out of the car the Lord spoke to me and said, "Thou shalt not tempt the Lord thy God." Wow! His mercy watched over us, but I was very glad to be home in one piece. I learned a lesson on faith versus presumption, though. (More about Jo later.)

Jerry's mother was not well, and he was an only child. We decided to move back to Danville to be near her if he could find work. Besides, the job in Indianapolis was not all that stable. Meanwhile Jerry had finished his Berean courses, and he was licensed in the Indiana District. However, shortly after getting his license he was called in and reprimanded for preaching in a church in Bloomington as a fill-in in a church that was not an Assembly of God Church. The Superintendent said he would have to make a choice.

Earlier we had an opportunity to try out for an Assembly church, but a leading woman felt that my bleached hair was not acceptable. I worked at a beauty shop, and it really threw me for a loop. Since we were moving back to Danville, it did not really matter. If we had been better communicator's it would have helped. We were very naive about church workings at that time. Also, in hindsight, we represented the charismatic renewal, good and bad. The kids were packed up again, and bless their hearts, they did not complain.

BACK TO ILLINOIS

Jerry got a job back in the factory he did not like, but it was a living. We found a house to rent in Oakwood. It was a miracle that we had no trouble renting with having all the kids. Most of the people that we considered friends went to the Rock Church. They were insisting that we go through catechism and be re baptized in Jesus Name. They said we could not be a part of the church if we refused to be baptized again because they did not accept being baptized in the name of the Father, Son and Holy Ghost. They believed that water baptism, properly administered cut away the enmity in your heart for holiness. The Lord spoke to me that it was an exclusive spirit.

The leaders at the Rock church then said we were not under a spiritual covering. We should have just ignored it and gone on, but it really hurt. I was not about to go along with a doctrine that I did not believe in. I knew the blood of Jesus had cleansed and changed me and that Jesus had imparted to me His righteousness. It took me several years to overcome the offense, and today, I would not let a difference like this affect me as much.

I wanted these people to accept me, and they did not. They were also very much against home meetings. The Shepherding Movement had begun which stressed being submissive to your pastor. The Rock church really believed this! Like everything else that is in the word, excess is dangerous. And in my opinion, it stifled the creative ministry of the Holy Spirit from using many local influential Christians who had very great potential to turn that area upside down for Jesus. The church was ingrown through those years.

We went to the Danville Assembly, and I helped the pastor's daughter start an Aglow, we had good meetings. She moved away, and I presided over the meetings for some time. It was fun and a highlight for me to be a part of this. I was asked to be a part of the State leadership, but just about that time, Jerry took a job in Fenton, Missouri. His mom was willing to move there with us.

TEACH AND BE TAUGHT IN MISSOURI

In Missouri, Jerry was much happier at his job and to be out of the factory. He had to do some traveling, but I think he enjoyed the quiet time. His boss was a screamer, but Jerry was able to have an influence on him, and his business partner became a Christian. It was also good for building Christian character in Jerry as he learned to maintain peace during his boss's tirades.

When we first moved to Missouri, we began attending an Assembly of God Church that was huge, and we really did not get to know anyone. However, I was able to lead my neighbor to the Lord, and she went there. Also, my boss at the beauty shop that I worked at and her husband began going there. I hungered for relationships with others in ministry.

We ended up going to Christian Outreach Center in Hillsboro, Mo. Bob Heil, a Pentecostal Lutheran pastor, had a church and Bible School on an old Catholic campground they had purchased. We had a heart for Christian community, and we heard this was that type of ministry. Many people lived either on the property or as close as they could get. They had a Christian school for the kids. Bob was also a board member for Aglow International, so I felt a kinship there. He had spoken at FGBMFI, so we had that contact, too.

We fit in, and they asked Jerry to teach Evangelism and Gifts of the Spirit in their Bible School. One interesting experience we had while working with the students in evangelism: We had a small outpost in Fenton where we preached, and Joyce Meyer attended one of our meetings. Of course, this was when she was just teaching her home Bible studies. She came up to Jerry afterwards and said she did not agree with him about a point. He had said God does not hear the prayers of sinners, except for repentance. It was a case of semantics. The ladies had great respect for her even then before her ministry took off. I also remember a couple of years later, Greg telling me that there was some lady on the St. Louis radio station (Joyce Meyer) who preached about as strong as I did. Today, I am honored at that comment.

Jerry also had opportunity to preach in Lutheran and Methodist churches during this time. People were hungry for teaching on the Holy Spirit. We saw the charismatic renewal spread, and some of these churches ended up with splits.

We preached in a lot of church basements and back rooms. It seems the pastors wanted the teaching, but they wanted to keep the Holy Spirit behind the scenes. While the pastors may desire this, once the people are filled with the Holy Spirit boldness comes that makes it hard to keep the fire on low. Jesus came to give his life that we might have eternal life. The Holy Spirit came to help us spread that message.

We used the Christian Outreach Center's tent to do outreaches, and some of the students went with us to do the music and morning teaching. We pitched the tent in Champaign, IL. and had a pretty good meeting. One man who received the baptism in the Holy Spirit at that meeting we learned had begun a charismatic church in Tolono. We were blessed when we heard that because Tolono is where our walk with Jesus began.

Charismatic Renewal

The Outreach Center also had a school for the children of the students and staff. Jason had trouble in kindergarten in public school, and when we put him in the Christian Outreach Center's School the following year, they worked wonders with him. Rachel began kindergarten there. The older boys went to public schools.

Most of the Center's leadership had Lutheran backgrounds, but many of the students were from Methodist and various other backgrounds. Most of them had families and had been converted as adults and then called into ministry. The COSM (Christian Outreach School of Ministry) was gaining a pretty wide recognition and the leaders were trying to get credentialed while we were there.

One group of COSM students, many whom had come out of the drug culture, had started a commune called Victory Farm which was located close by. Some of the leaders were from good Lutheran families and others had been very deep into drugs before conversion to Christ. When we had been at COC a few years, the group from the Farm asked us to come and work with them. We had done some tent meetings with the students and were anxious to be in full time ministry. We thought this might be God's leading.

It probably was. It was here that we got hands-on training for later mission work. There had been some falling out because of the way that the Victory Farm group had started their own ministry, and the Lord used us a little in renewing fellowship. I had all the ladies from Christian Outreach Center along with the ladies from Victory Farm for a gathering after we moved, and it was a good time. I did not think anything about it but learned later it meant a lot to them and helped renew friendships.

Victory Farm basically took in troubled youth, and it was a discipleship program ran more like Christian community. Everyone had their chores, and there were classes to go to. I didn't get too involved because I was busy with my own kids. Greg had just graduated from high school, and he had a girlfriend. The leaders did not like it if he stayed out late. I did not really blame them, but I could not lock Greg up either. Our poor kids had been shoved around way too much. It is God's grace that Greg is serving the Lord in St. Louis today with his wife and kids.

I'll admit it. I was too spoiled to stay at the farm. I really liked the ladies, but I felt out of the loop somewhat or maybe it was that the rigid structure began to wear on me. Before we had moved to St. Louis, the Lord had spoken to me that we would teach and be taught. That word surely came to pass.

One of the strong points of the Bible School, and the church service at COC was praise and worship. In the early seventies they were on the cutting edge for choreographed dance, and the worship team was wonderful. Some of those students went on to work for Integrity Music, had music ministries, and many are pastors around the country. Another leader at Christian Outreach Center was Lynn Haitz, who was a Charismatic Lutheran minister in his sixties who was a missionary into all kinds of places that many missionaries would never go. The students who felt called to missions learned from him.

A young couple, who left very lucrative professions, came down to work with him and organized an adoption plan. They raised funds for many impoverished children that Lynn met through his travels. The children were adopted for so much a month by various families around the country. While at COC we also learned how to do bulk mailings and other fundraising techniques that we needed to know later.

Many of the students at Christian Outreach Center had given up jobs to come to Missouri and go to Bible School so they could serve the Lord in ministry. We did water baptize a few who had only been sprinkled as babies. It was a controversial subject at the school as many still held to infant baptism. However, it did not divide the camp.

OUR WORK AS HOME MISSIONARIES

We felt like the Lord was calling us back to Danville to begin a street outreach to youth.

I came home first and stayed with my sister Judy for a week before Jerry came back with his mom. I brought Jason and Rachel with me and the older boys came with Jerry. Greg, our oldest was out of high school, and he wanted to stay in Missouri.

We were able to rent two apartments, one for us, and one for his mother. One good thing, the apartment had a swimming pool which made the move easier on the boys. They adjusted without complaint. The Women Aglow group had become very small. The women wanted me to take it over again and I tried, but I could not get it back on track. I felt so bad about it because the officers loved God but could not see that their actions were acceptable maybe for a real Pentecostal prayer meeting but not for a Women's Outreach Meeting.

It was happening in Aglow Chapters everywhere. They seemed to have trouble having an outreach meeting and were focusing more on prayer. Prayer is always good, but it was not the calling of Women's Aglow Meetings. It was raised up to bring women into the Baptism of the Holy Spirit and salvation through the vehicle of testimonies. Many Chapters went into churches or small meeting rooms to save on costs.

In the seventies this organization was used mightily of

God. But later many women had fellowship in their own churches as the new charismatic churches formed. Many Aglow chapters are doing other types of good works in the name of the Lord, and the organization is still in existence. It was a true blessing to me in the early years of my walk with the Lord.

Some friends from Rossville and I had a Charismatic Women's Conference in a Methodist Church and women from around the area attended, except for the women from the Rock. I was disappointed denominational walls were up again. However, women from around the area came, and new people were exposed to the gospel and to the truth about the baptism in the Spirit. Our main speakers were Betty Clem and Barbara Kehoe from Ball State University. Their husbands were part of the faculty at the university, and both couples had dynamic testimonies and were greatly used in the Charismatic renewal. Barbara's daughter had been in a diving accident and had been paralyzed, but as they stood on the word, and the Lord healed her daughter against all odds.

When we became Christian it was nothing like today with Charismatic churches in practically every town. Dennis Bennet, an Episcopalian Minister, wrote a book about his experience with the Holy Spirit called <u>Nine O'clock in the Morning.</u> These testimonial books along with testimonial books put out by FGBMFI were tools that helped spread the spiritual awakening into various mainline churches. In time many were led to begin new churches. This is the same way the Assemblies of God formed in 1914. People were forced to leave their old churches when they received the Baptism in the Holy Spirit. They had the need to form new churches and they formed the Assemblies of God to better coordinated their missionary support and training. Now many of the new charismatic churches have joined with others and are basically the same structure as any other denomination. This is not wrong if we maintain an open heart to God's Spirit.

We attended the Danville First Assembly of God church. Jerry worked at the apartment complex where we lived, and we worked at holding some evangelistic meetings. We wanted to teach evangelism clinics, much the way that the Methodist Lay Witness program worked. It was more of a hands-on training on personal evangelism, than preaching. It involved teaching workshops, and it incorporated a fellowship meal along with small group participation. It really was a neat idea. We were able to hold a couple, but they never did really take off. We still were considered outsiders by our charismatic friends because we did not attend the Rock. Because the Rock was influential, our unpopularity went even farther. That on top of the Aglow not working made for a sad time. However, we felt the Lord called us back to Danville to establish a street outreach ministry, and we began promoting the idea wherever we could. Our Assemblies of God pastor seemed to be behind the idea.

We had a fundraising dinner and invited a converted ex-drag queen we knew from Missouri to be the speaker. It drew a pretty good crowd, and we had a good contemporary music group. This group ended up playing at the coffee house when we originally established the ministry, but that was a year and a half later. Our pastor told us about a campground sitting empty about fifteen miles out of town near Potomac, Illinois. Shades of Victory Farm!

THE WESTCOVE PROPERTY

Westcove was a forty- acre property with several buildings on it. It had been a private Christian High School but had closed for lack of students. It had been vacated for several years and was in need of repairs. A young family from Christian Outreach Center, Chuck and Sue and their two children, came to help us. We began to get people sent to us for the program that we had put together. The program was much like what we did at Victory Farm in Missouri. We also had a couple of church retreats to help bring in some finances. The property had a lot of potential, but it we did not have enough finances coming in.

The owners gave us grace and helped by paying the utilities, but we got very weary of the financial strain of it all. The Danville newspaper had put an article in the paper about the ministry where they quoted us as saying we were "like" a Teen Challenge. A local minister complained to Carlinville, our denominations headquarters, that we were using the Teen Challenge name wrongly. The name of our ministry was Midwest Christian Training Center, so we know that it was an attack of the enemy. However, our pastor at Danville Assembly was no longer interested in the ministry, and when Jerry went to the office, he had been given in the church administration building he found the locks had been changed. They said it was because we called ourselves a Teen Challenge when we were not.

We hosted a couple of retreats for churches, and I

had a ladies retreat, while at the Westcove property. I invited my friend Jo, from Indianapolis, to come and speak at the ladies retreat. When we first moved back to Danville, I had heard on the evening news that her husband had died while out jogging, and I wanted to stay in touch. She told me the Faith church they had been under not only did not believe in doctors, but they also did not believe in insurance.

Jo's husband provided well when he was alive, but finances dried up quickly. It was a hard time for Jo with three boys in college. She had not worked in years, and even though she had a college degree, she struggled to find a job. She found one, and she had a couple come share her house with her to help with that upkeep. She learned Social Security would cover the boy's education. God was seeing her through day by day.

The reason I included her story is that it is so interesting to see what the Lord did in her life! A year or so later she was introduced to a man who was an International Director in Full Gospel in England. They fell in love and when she mailed me a picture of her house, it was an English manor that probably covered an acre of ground. They were able to spend time ministering and enjoying their families together, traveling back and forth across the globe. God is good! Jo and I were able to meet for lunch at a later time, and she said the women in England are much more subdued and genteel. I could tell a difference in her, but she still had a zeal for Jesus.

During that time at Westcove, we made friends with our neighbors who were farmers with property behind us. They had some misgivings about the types of people we might be ministering to. There had been some problems in the neighborhood with the High School students who had been at Westcove property before us. However, this young couple soon became a part of the ministry, along with their parents who were a great help and became board members for the ministry. They became Spirit-filled and today they belong to Living Word Fellowship in St. Joseph. While at Westcove, we met with their weekly Bible study that gathered in various homes in that area, and we met some really nice people.

Good things came out of our time at Westcove, but it was a stressful time because of finances. I found out that I was pregnant again. At that time, it was not common for forty-year old women to have babies. When I went to the doctor, he wanted me to consider whether I wanted to carry the baby. Being against abortion, I was furious that he would suggest such a thing and determined to not go back. I thought maybe I could have the baby at home to save money. After all I had five children with no complications, and it was getting to be common among Christians to have babies at home with midwives. A lady from Danville said she would help, but her only experience was reading books and having seven children of her own. Having children and delivering babies is two different things!

We decided to leave Westcove, and it was a hard time for us and the couple who was on staff. I felt so bad for them. They went back to Missouri to Christian Outreach Center and later joined the Foursquare Church where they were pastors for many years. We moved to an empty farmhouse close to Westcove in Ellis. It is a town of three houses, but one nice thing is the other house had children for Rachel and Jason to play with. Brad and Charles continued to go to Armstrong High School. They were blessed to have jobs at the school working on the janitorial staff. The man who owned the house we rented owned a grain elevator, and he hired Jerry. God was faithful in the fact that we always have had our needs met.

It is a miracle, and we give God all the glory.

I prayed as the vision for ministry certainly had not left. While in this rented house, I put together better guidelines and plans for a ministry that would disciple and help people who found themselves homeless but open to Christian discipleship. From our time at Westcove, we could see that there were young people who were homeless, and that there was a need in that area.

Meanwhile it came time to have my baby, and when it came time to deliver, the lady who was supposed to help deliver panicked. I ended up going to the hospital in an ambulance. The poor kids were scared and so was Jerry. The ambulance driver and his helper said they could deliver the baby, but by then I wanted the security of a hospital. Since I did not have a regular doctor, a doctor had to come in from a party, and he was not very happy. However, he had compassion on me, and ended up not charging me. One good thing that came out of the hospital visit is that my roommate came to know the Lord, and we became friends. Sarah was born, and she has been a great blessing to us. Sarah means "princess" and she has always been the princess in the family. As much as four brothers will let her be.

Jerry answered an ad for Quaker Oats for a supervisory position, and he got it. We were so happy to have good money coming in for the first time in a long time. We heard that the old Elks building had been bought by a Christian businessman in Tulsa and was for sale for only $7,000. We were so excited. It was the perfect location for the ministry. After about six months of politics with the Danville city council and the businessman, we gave up on the building.

We did hear from another Christian businessman that there was a four-plex for sale at 404 Gilbert Street which we could have if we would just take over the payments. It was a good location and each apartment had about 1200 square feet. We moved into it and stuck a sign out in front that said Midwest Christian Training Center. We had a board of directors and our 501(c) 3 from the federal government.

Opposition? We had criticism from several Christian leaders who said we were not under spiritual covering. We felt like lone rangers and I guess we were. The Assembly pastor who had ostracized us for the "Teen Challenge" mix-up, left to work for TBN with Rev. Dortch, but we were not sure we wanted to go back to the Assembly. The Rock church still wanted us to go through catechism and be re-baptized, and we did not feel right about that either, so we attended the Methodist church on the corner.

People told us that the Church of God pastor also criticized us for not being "under a covering" which kept us from going that direction. However, he moved away, and Jim and Mary Ford took over that church. They were two of our best friends during our next years in Danville, and they were a real encouragement in helping us get the mission established. Today I would confront those rumors but at that time I allowed offenses to enter in. Jerry managed to live above it all. Meanwhile many people did support our ministry, and I worked at developing it as best I could.

We had a home meeting with some of the young people who had played music at our fundraiser when we first came back to Danville. We decided to have a coffee house outreach in the new building. It was a lot of fun, and an odd assortment of young teens and adults would come on Friday and Saturday nights. Laurie, one of the musician's wives, decorated the rooms like a Hippie

Hangout, and people donated card tables for us to use. We had some other contemporary groups in occasionally. My kids were a great help with serving and cleaning up.

The Quetone's came on staff to help us. They were "Friends" background, but she had graduated from Oral Roberts University in music. She had a beautiful singing voice. She was into health food and had all her babies delivered at home. I respected them, and they were willing to pitch in and help in all ways. They were good helping at the coffee house. They were friends with a spirit-filled Methodist pastor and his wife, who also joined our board. Later, we held an Evangelism Clinic in his church in the heights and the Christian Church across the road from his. Several received the baptism in the Holy Spirit, and that church has continued to support the mission.

We decided to have an outdoor concert with one of the well-known contemporary praise bands from Indianapolis. In fact, my friend Jo's son from Indianapolis was in the band. There was an empty lot across from the ministry building, which was located on Gilbert Street, and so we decided to have it there. That night the entire area filled with people and it looked which like an outdoor festival. The music was loud, but the message was clear. Jesus is Lord! It was a great night, except that the police came by and gave us a talking to for not getting a permit. As usual with Christian outreaches the crowd was well behaved and there was no trouble.

I also had some ladies luncheon meetings in the coffee house and had various speakers come in that I had met through Women Aglow. Again, I marvel at how God supplied all our needs during those early years in the mission ministry. Becky Quetone helped with those meetings, and her music ministry was a great blessing. She had a professional traditional sound, but all ages enjoyed her music, and there was a real anointing on it. The Lord really moved in those meetings, and we saw souls saved.

It was hard on my oldest son Charles to change schools, and he fell in with some kids who were not a good influence. We should have seen it coming. He met a girl and married her at age 18. A rough three years followed as the relationship did not work out. We take much of the blame for that period in his life. A baby girl named Jennifer, our first grandchild, was born. Charles later married a Christian girl and it is hard to remember those days. I thank the Lord for Brook who has been a good helpmate for him, and they have a good life today, thanks to God's grace. I am proud of how all my kids have turned out. The older ones were uprooted way too much. They are a blessing to us today, along with their spouses and the grandchildren we have. The only stable factor they had for those years was that we loved them, and we loved Jesus.

The Danville Salvation Army did not house people over night, so they contacted us to see if we would take in people, and they would pay us. Meanwhile we made friends with the director of the Galesburg Rescue Mission, Ernie and Pat Kline became good friends of ours. She was active in the Galesburg Aglow, and they loved Jesus. We learned from them, and we also visited several large city missions around the state to see how they did things. We found that we already had more of a program than many of them offered. However, we did learn a lot, and we began to go to conventions that featured all aspects of support ministries to Rescue Missions.

We joined International Union of Gospel Missions. This organization had new leadership, and many of the city missions grew tremendously during these years. They began to hire outside fund raisers and hire professional staff. Before that time few mission workers had advanced degrees. While most of these missionaries are not Pentecostal, they are born-again, and we met very loving and caring people through that fellowship of believers. We felt a kindred spirit with the people in IUGM just like we did our other friends in this type of ministry.

I believe that it was during this time that the charismatic move began to ebb. I prayed in the Holy Spirit, because I believe it is the only way to have the peace of God in my life. The Bible says that we are edified through this kind of prayer, and personally, I have found that for my mental and emotional wellbeing it is vital that I pray in the Spirit. Many times in my life this relationship with the Lord through the Holy Spirit has been my anchor against Satan's attacks.

Going to a full-gospel church and participating in a group that moves in the Holy Spirit are two different things, and I believe that we all need to be in a smaller group, also. The mission gave us the day to day fellowship we had experienced in the charismatic movement.

Many of the homeless people who stayed at the mission also gave their lives to the Lord. However, we saw more backsliding than we had ever seen before, and the commitments were often more shallow. It is the nature of that type of ministry. However, over the years, we saw God stabilize many of those who made commitments to Jesus. It was just a long process rather than a radical change like the testimonies we heard in Full Gospel.

When the Bible says to raise a child in the way in which they should go and when they are old, they shall not depart from it. That principal can also work in the negative. When children have been abused it takes time sometimes for God's grace to help them overcome those emotional scars. Mr. and Mrs. Martin Wegehaupt were board members during this time. They were an older Lutheran couple who we had met through the Full Gospel Businessmen's meetings. They were both retired schoolteachers, and they were a tremendous help at the ministry.

The Commercial News did several articles on our work and we began to be more financially stable. The city leaders were glad we were there. The pastors from the Rock Church came to visit and apologized for any wrongs they had done toward us. In the years that followed they loosened up on their doctrine and accepted us into their fellowship without our being baptized again. At that time, we accepted their apology and were glad they had contacted us, but we were aware that our reputation had been hurt in many Charismatic quarters by the spiritual covering doctrine.

We sold the apartment building and moved downtown to the old Township Building. Our ministry flourished there, and Jerry decided to quit his job to be full-time director. We had another couple helping us now who we had met at Christian Outreach Center. This couple made friends with a couple who along with some prominent Christian businessmen decided to start another mission. The man had been a mission director in Terre Haute. The Lord protected us from being aware of what was going on until it was over with. Some people's consciences kicked in, and they ended up beginning a different type of work instead.

After a year in the Township building, the bank next door wanted our property for a drive-through banking facility. They put a lot of pressure on us to sell them the building. We learned about power within the city! Anyway, we bought the Fairchild School building on Bowman Avenue for $65,000. It was a real struggle for a year or two, because the heat bills were over a thousand dollars a month.

We hosted a convention for International Union of Gospel Missions, and Steve Burger who was the International president came. We felt honored to hold the convention. Greg and Kathy helped us. Our oldest son, Greg had moved back home to Illinois long enough to meet Kathy Moore from my hometown of Rossville. They worked with us a short time and then moved back to Missouri. Charles also worked with us for a short time. They were good workers. Greg had vision, and Charles was very conscientious. He kept the mission cleaner than anyone since then. We were pleased that the Assembly and the Rock began to support the ministry on a monthly basis.

There was a gym in the middle of the mission building, and we were able to have a children's outreach one night a week. We picked up kids from the local housing project and children came from the Lutheran School that the girls went to as well as some neighborhood children. We had some good turnouts, but more came than we could handle, and we could not recruit enough workers. Mrs. Wegehaupt and Sherri Huff helped, and it was a good ministry. To me, there is no greater ministry than children's ministry, especially when the children are from dysfunctional homes. The church can be a surrogate family, and that is what we are called to be.

Many churches have lost their burden for child evangelism, and I wonder if they forget that hell is real, and that even little children must be led to repentance. I often hear people talk like all children are going to heaven. Jesus said that narrow is the way.

That narrow way is through a covenant relationship with Jesus Christ and his shed blood. A child is sanctified through the faith of the parent. I Corinthians 7:14, Malachi 2:15 states the importance of covenant relationship with God and that includes children. Original sin was debated in the fifty century and the Council of Ephesus in 431 condemned the fact that children are born without a sin nature,

Humanism and today's culture have affected the thinking of many believers. Before I was born-again my mind had to be renewed to see that a loving God is a just God, and that the only way for our sins to be removed is through accepting Jesus. We must see a renewal of child evangelism, and we must pray for their parents to come into the kingdom. Jerry and I shudder to think of where our family would be if we had not met Jesus when we did.

Jerry organized a food basket drive for Thanksgiving, and the mission was able to give away close to seven hundred food baskets each year during that season. We were able to share the gospel with many of these families. We always shared the gospel with the groups that came in for free clothes or food, and the people always seemed to enjoy it. We rarely had a negative response to the gospel message. Repentance did not always follow, but at least they were respectful to the building and message.

We had some trying instances. We had bought Rachel a cocker spaniel puppy, and it got stolen. When the mission was on Gilbert Street, someone stole a Moped and bicycle of Brad's. That was a heartbreaker because he was sixteen at the time and had worked hard to buy them. We later found out that friends of one of the tenants we were having a hard time moving out had taken them. We wanted these people to move out so that we could have room for the ministry, and they were three months behind on their rent. When they finally did move out, they tried to steal the appliances. Later when we had moved the mission to Fairchild School, that tenant came in for assistance. We helped her, but I thought that the Lord does not bless the wicked.

We had one man who had been in prison much of his life. He was a good cook, and he worked in the mission's kitchen. Early one morning Jerry went down to the dining hall and there was a ruckus. After he stepped between the two men, Jerry realized one had a knife. He did not get cut but Rufus did, and we had to call the police. It was the only real danger we ever were aware of.

Our guidelines did not allow anyone in the mission who had been drinking, and that kept a lot of trouble out. That one guideline was what made for a safe mission. Non-Christian city missions do not have that rule, and many homeless people will not stay in those missions because they are not safe. Is it any wonder that we believe Christians should abstain from alcohol? We had some tremendous helpers at the mission who the Lord delivered from alcohol.

We also had a half-way house contract with the Federal government for a while. Some of the men who came through were white collar workers, bankers, etc. We hoped that the gospel message ministered to them, but when they left, we did not hear from them again. It was a season in their lives they wanted to put behind them I am sure. We also had a contract for a short time with the State, but we found those men did not fit into the program as well and we dropped it.

Along with the Matta's and Fords, we helped to form

Charismatic Renewal

a local Jesus March that drew a large crowd into a local park. We did this for two years, and many joined with us the second year including the Rock. Unity was beginning to manifest among the Pentecostals. The meeting was an appeal to repent, especially for abortion. We had pro-life speakers, and the mayor and others spoke on many issues that Christians needed to be addressed. It was a large public prayer time. We had music, banners, etc. At least we took Jesus outside the four walls of the church building.

The supernatural wave called the Charismatic renewal was over in the United States. The church statistics tell us that most church growth is now transfer growth, and the numbers of new converts is not increasing. That Holy Spirit move where thousands were receiving the Baptism in the Holy Spirit and new converts were coming to know Jesus has stopped and ministry had been largely relegated back to the church building.

We saw the Lord establish Danville Rescue Mission, and Jerry worked in that field of ministry as Executive Director in missions in Indianapolis and Huntsville, Al. In 1998 Jerry left mission work to pastor in Assembly churches in Charleston and Paris, IL. We spent one year as Regional Missionaries on the East Coast for US MAPS, a division of the Assemblies of God. That year of service gave us a great appreciation for the Assemblies U. S. Missionaries working on our campuses and in the inner cities.

THE WIND OF THE SPIRIT CHANGES

However, it seems that the real sovereign move of God, the wave of the Spirit or the Charismatic movement began to ebb in the mid-eighties, and while many churches were beginning and many were receiving the Baptism in the Holy Spirit, church surveys tell us that much of the growth was transferring from one church to another rather than new lost souls coming into the kingdom. For a time, thousands were coming to know the Lord daily, just like in the book of Acts.

We have had our tests as we have endeavored to follow Jesus and the path that He was leading us in. He has opened doors for us, and many times we have been rejected by men. That is all just a part of the walk of a disciple. Jesus said if they persecute me, they will persecute you also. The Lord has spoken to my heart that we must love at all costs and rejoice in Jesus. We must keep our eyes on Jesus, the Lord of the harvest. The Christian life has been a great life because we are complete only in Him.

A NEW WAVE

I just returned home from "THE CALL" a prayer meeting held in Nashville, Tennessee July 7, 07. It was exciting to see over 75,000 people in the Titian's stadium praying for our nation. There was repentance for all the sins, prejudice and sexual sins, etc. It makes me very sad to think that the great charismatic revival that we were a part of did not have a greater impact on the last generation and the culture we live in. The world has gotten far worse over the past forty years. The media has regressed in a shocking manner. The video games, school violence, etc. has mushroomed. However, I sense the wind of revival, another wave coming. Each wave is different as this generation is different, but some things are the same. God still demands holiness, and he demands consecration. The theme of the CALL was to prepare for the coming Bridegroom King. God is calling us to a greater intimacy with Him. The music at the CALL was not praise bands, but musicians leading us into adoration, focusing on the face of Jesus.

I was blessed to have my daughter Sarah there with her husband. She is seven months pregnant with her first child. I remembered being at the March for Jesus in 1980 in Washington D.C. when I was pregnant with her! Some things never change. Unlike Sarah, I did not wear a tank top, with my baby belly showing, and times change in some ways. My oldest son Greg, his wife Kathy and their six boys were there from St. Louis. A new generation, a new wave of the Spirit is beginning to happen.

A prophecy given at the CALL spoke to me. It was that God is going to pour out a supernatural outpouring of His love on the church.

I remembered an old prophecy from years ago that has not been fulfilled. God told us that things were going to get worse and worse in the world but better and better in the church. Things have gotten worse in the world since the time of that prophecy, but they have not really gotten better in the church.

However, I see this even now beginning to happen. God's love is beginning to flow in a greater measure, and there is nothing that will make the body of Christ better than His love flowing among us. The early church had this. People are drawn by His loving kindness flowing thought us. People are again meeting in homes, desiring accountability and real relationships within the body of Christ. I John 5:2 teaches us that God's love comes with obedience to His commandments. That is the only unity that brings God's love on the scene. We may never be perfect in this body, but we will be quick to repent, and we will not justify sin if we expect to see His glory manifest.

Someone said at the CALL that The FEAR OF THE LORD is our BANNER. The Lord gave me a scripture out of Jeremiah about judgment. I believe that we need to reverence, respect and be in awe of the Lord. In the book of John Jesus said that he came to judge the earth. Judgment will begin in the household of God. If we repent and remain in short accounts with our Lord, we do not need to worry about judgment. But judgment will come to the household of God.

Today, we are pastors of a small church in Paris, Illinois. Our greatest desire is to be open to what the Holy Spirit is doing and move with God. Jesus is coming soon, and this is a generation that is in desperate need of revival. We should all hope to have an impact that will change the lives of the next generation.

The sin of the last move was that too many were self-seeking. If we want to change the culture this cannot be. The house church movement and cell groups are picking up speed. We know we must have relationships that focus on the Holy Spirit, or Jesus, which is more important than what structures we use. Some ministries are bold in their witnessing outside the church. When Jesus said to minister the gospel to the poor, it is because they are much more open to the gospel in the poor neighborhoods. There people will stop and listen. In the suburbs security systems lock up possessions and lock out the gospel. There is a harvest to be reaped, but we must go and bring it in.

I read in Malachi chapters three and four that God is going to use those people who love Him and talk often about Him as his special vessels in the day in which He shall act. Jesus is coming back….Our Bridegroom, King. Maranatha…Come quickly Lord Jesus.

A Foot Note

Fast forward to 2014: I had mentioned a grandson with an incurable disease. He is fourteen years old and fully recovered. The tent-evangelist that had fallen away is back preaching the gospel. God desires for us all to not be weary in well-doing for we will reap if we faint not. He has a plan for every one of us, and it is a joy to connect with fellow believers as we work together to bring in the harvest in these last days.

The Four Spiritual Laws

(Condensed form)

Just as there are physical laws that govern the physical universe, so are there spiritual laws that govern your relationship with God.

1. Law Number One: God loves you and has a wonderful plan for your life.

   John 10:10 "I have come that you might have life and that more abundantly."

2. Law Number Two: Man is sinful and separated from God. Therefore, he cannot know and experience God's love and plan for his life.

   Romans 3:23 "For ALL have sinned and fall short of the glory of God."

3. Law Number Three: Jesus Christ is God's only provision for man's sin. Through Him you can know and experience God's love and plan for your life.

   Romans 5:8 "God demonstrates His own love toward us, in that while we were yet sinners, Christ died for us."

4. Law Number Four: We must individually receive

Jesus Christ as Savior and Lord; then we can know and experience God's love and plan for our lives.

John 1:12 "As many as RECEIVED Him, to them He gave the right to become children of God, even to those who believe in His name."

Holy Spirit Baptism

Jesus said for you to receive this experience:

"Behold, I send the Promise of my Father upon you, but tarry in the city of Jerusalem until you are endued with power from on high." Luke 24:50 This was Jesus' last instruction before ascending to the Father.

"But you shall receive power after that the Holy Ghost is come upon you, and ye shall be witnesses unto me in Jerusalem, and in all Judea and Samaria, and to the end of the world." Acts 1:8

John the Baptist also said, "I indeed baptize you with water, but One mightier than I is coming, whose sandal strap I am not worthy to loose. He will baptize you with the Holy Spirit and fire." Luke 3:16 He was speaking of Jesus

Examples in the Book of Acts:

Read these scriptural accounts, and it will build your faith!

> On the day of Pentecost...............Acts 2:4
> At Cornelius's House.................Acts 10:44-46
> The Ephesians believers............Acts 19:6
> The Samaritan Receive...............Acts 8:14-17

What are the requirements to receiving the Baptism in the Holy Spirit?

You must be saved. (Acts 2:38-39)

You must receive by asking in faith. (Luke 11:10-13)

You must desire to do the works of Jesus

and be his witness. (John 14:12)

Why Tongues?

A. For edification. It builds you up spiritually.

"He who speaks in a tongue edifies himself." I Corinthians 14:4

"But you, beloved, building yourselves up in your most holy faith, praying in the Holy Spirit," Jude 20

B. For Prayer.

"Likewise, the Spirit helps us in our weakness; for we do not know how to pray as we ought, but the Spirit himself intercedes for us with sighing's too deep for words." Romans 8:26

"For if I pray in a tongue, my spirit prays, but my understanding is unfruitful. What is the conclusion then? I will pray with the spirit, and I will pray with the understanding." I Corinthians 14:14-15

C. It was promised through the Old Testament prophets.

Isaiah 28:11-12, Joel 2:28-32, Psalms 8:2

Ask and Receive:

"For all the promises of God in Him are yea, and in Him amen, unto the glory of God by us." II Corinthians 1:20

"This only I want to learn from you: Did you receive the Spirit by the works of the law, or by the hearing of faith?" Galatians 3:2

~ ~ ~

www.ingramcontent.com/pod-product-compliance
Lightning Source LLC
Chambersburg PA
CBHW031454040426
42444CB00007B/1093